MIDLAND
A to Z

MIDLAND
A to Z

The History and Culture of Midland for Young Readers

Jimmy Patterson &
Karen J. Patterson

Abilene Christian University Press

MIDLAND A TO Z

The History and Culture of Midland for Young Readers

ACU
PRESS

Copyright © 2018 by Jimmy Patterson and Karen J. Patterson

ISBN 978-0-89112-413-9

Printed in the United States of America

Cover and interior text design by Sandy Armstrong, Strong Design

For information contact:
Abilene Christian University Press
ACU Box 29138
Abilene, Texas 79699

1-877-816-4455
www.acupressbooks.com

18 19 20 21 22 23 / 7 6 5 4 3 2 1

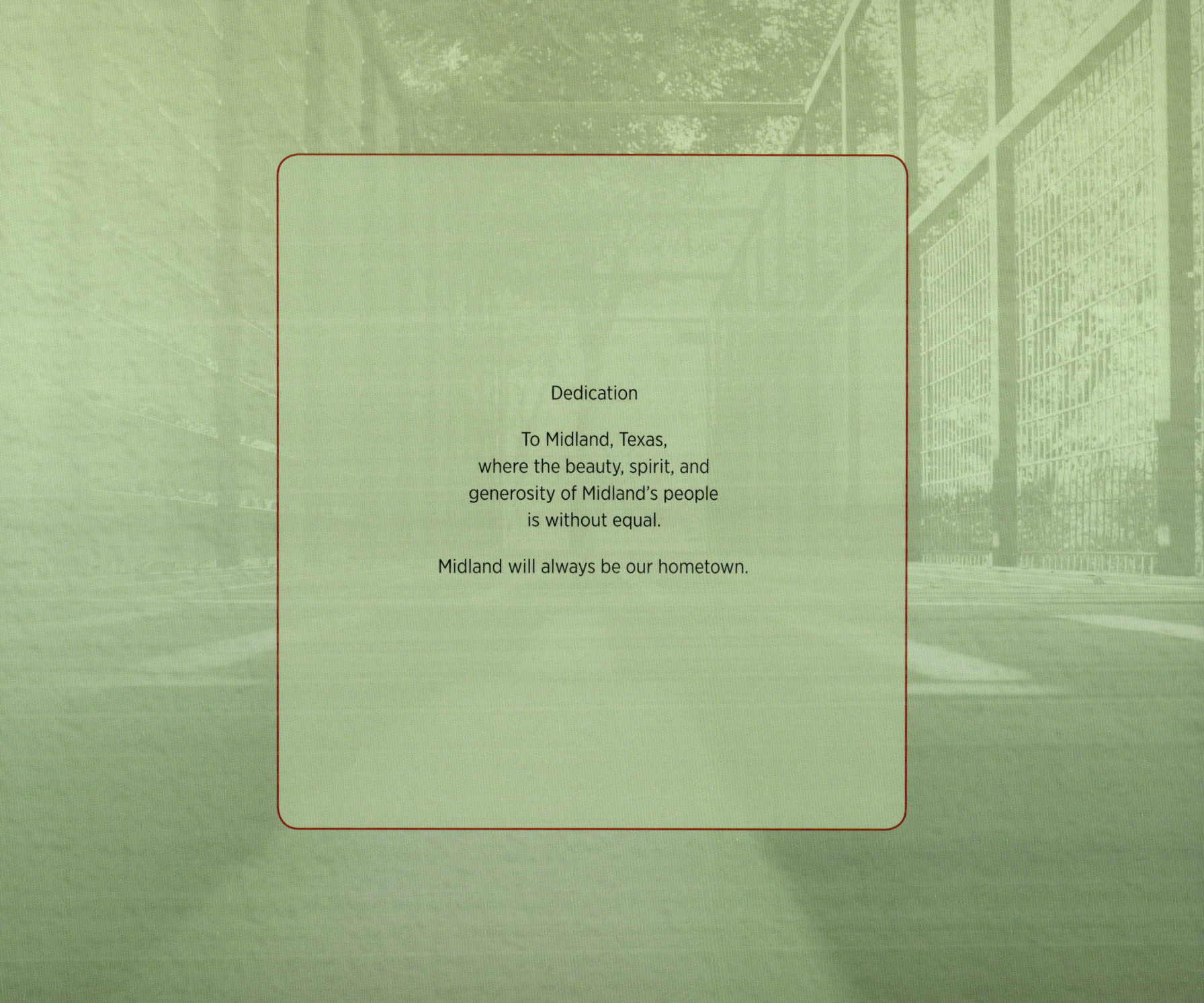

Dedication

To Midland, Texas,
where the beauty, spirit, and
generosity of Midland's people
is without equal.

Midland will always be our hometown.

Photo Credits

Unless otherwise noted, all photographs were taken by Karen J. Patterson.

Additionally, the publisher would like to thank the following
for their kind permission to reproduce their photographs/images.

Rafael Aguilera—Bellus Photo: Museum of the Southwest Ribbon Cutting K1. **Bill Brine**: [Public domain] Kentucky Derby field via Wikimedia Commons K2. **Brett Billings**: [Public domain] Monarch Butterfly via Pixnio I1a. **George W. Bush Childhood Home**: Bush building a snowman B2b; Home Opening B1b; Both Presidents B2; House B1c. **Aaron Easton**: Pliska Plane A1b. **EriKolaborator**: [Public domain] Planta Rodadora via Wikimedia Commons W2a. **Fiddlesticks Farm**: Welcome Z2; Hayride Z1; Pig Race Z2a; Corn Maze Design Z1b. **Veronica Galindo**: Alter C2a. **Haley Memorial Library and History Center**: Front H2; Research Room H1. **Carol M. Highsmith**: [Public domain] Windmill via Wikimedia Commons W1. **Steve Hillebrand**: [Public domain] Lizard via Pixnio I2a. **George Hodan**: [Public domain] Night Sky with Large Moon via Public Domain Photos M2b; Stars in the Night Sky S2c. **Judge John Hyde Family**: Judge John Hyde J2; Judge Hyde Volunteering J2a; Historic Midland County Courthouse J1. **Renji Shino:** [Public Domain] Tumbleweed via Wikimedia Commons W2a. **Midland International Air & Space Port**: Logo A2a. **Midland County Public Library**: Bookmobile L2c. **Midland RockHounds**: Rocky & Juice R2a; Play at Home-Good R1; Third Base Side R2. **Lettie Morrow**: Thomas Building D2a; Petroleum Building D2b; Cardinal I2c; Yellow Plant I2; Path I2b; Entrance I1; Museum of the Southwest M1a; Reporter Telegram N2; Newspaper Stand N1a; Park P2; Skatepark P2a; Doug Russell Park P1; Midland Sign Q1b; A Thursday Sunset S2; Friendship Sign U2; Cross U1; Vietnam Veterans Memorial V2; Chris Kyle Memorial V1b; Vietnam Veterans Statue V1c; Vietnam Veterans Quote V2a; Plant in Rocks X1; Rocks at the Cross X2; Cactus Flower X2b; Yucca Theatre Y2; Windmill at Park photo credit page. **Museum of the Southwest**: 1987 Kentucky Derby Trophy K2a. **Permian Basin Petroleum Museum**: Permian Sea O1; Energy City Timeline1. **Pedro Sanchez**: Passing the Ball F1; Entering the Field F2a. **Wayne Stratton Photography, waynestratton.com**: Lee vs MHS 3 Timeline2; Lee vs MHS 4 F2a. **H.G. Symonds Photos**: Sandstorm Passed over Midland TX Feb 2, 1984 at 6 P.M. Q1c.

Photo Location Key

1=Left; 2=Right
a=above; c=center; b=below

Airport

A is for Airport. Midland's first airport opened almost 100 years ago.

Hanging from the ceiling above baggage claim is the Pliska Plane, built by John Pliska and his assistant, Gray Coggin, in 1912. Mr. Pliska was inspired by the Wright Brothers. The Pliska Plane is an open-cockpit aircraft with a 33-foot-long wingspan and a 27.5-foot-long fuselage.

Midland International Air & Space Port

The Midland Air and Space Port is the first commercial spaceport to be located in a major U.S. airport. It is equipped with suborbital launching and landing corridors. One day in the future, tourists could blast off from Midland into outer space.

Bush Family

B is for the Bush family.
Two of America's presidents
lived in Midland!

In the 1950s, George H. W. and Barbara Bush moved to West Texas because of the jobs available in the oil business. George H. W. Bush became the 41st president of the United States on January 20, 1989.

One of the most popular places to visit in Midland is the George W. Bush Childhood Home at 1412 West Ohio Avenue, where you can hear the story of one of America's great families.

"W," as he is fondly referred to by many, lived in Midland as a child and later returned to West Texas as an adult to begin an oil business in the 1970s. While back in West Texas, he met and married Laura Welch, who became the First Lady of the United States when George W. Bush served as the 43rd president, from 2001–2008.

Churches

C is for churches. There are more than 175 churches in Midland.

In 1957, the First Christian Church in Midland was destroyed by a fire. Church members held a worship service while the church still smoldered around them. People from other churches donated hymnals, pews, and communion items so that the congregation could still have services after the fire.

The First Christian Church has very interesting architecture, including beautiful stained glass windows. Have you ever seen a stained glass window?

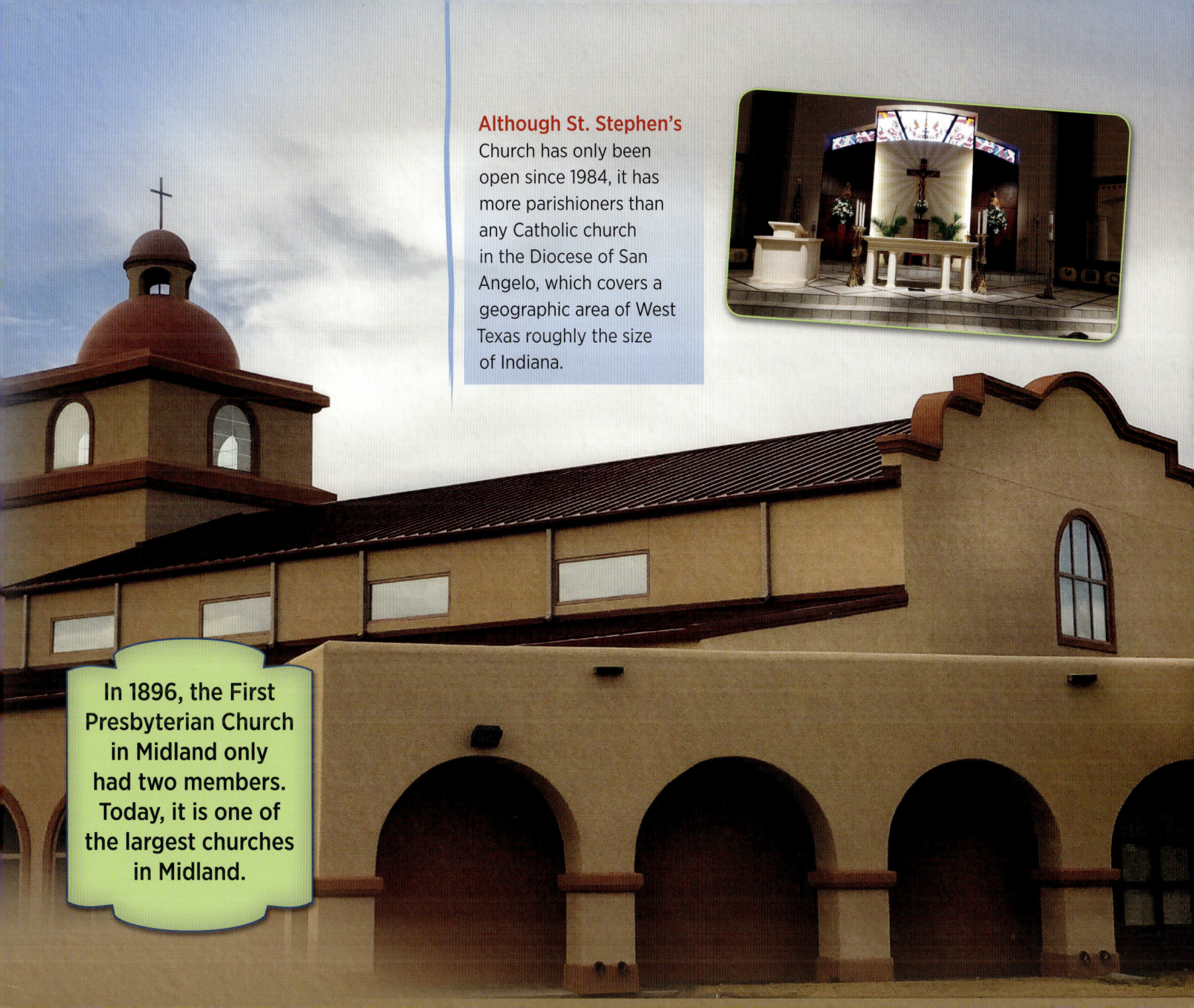

Although St. Stephen's Church has only been open since 1984, it has more parishioners than any Catholic church in the Diocese of San Angelo, which covers a geographic area of West Texas roughly the size of Indiana.

In 1896, the First Presbyterian Church in Midland only had two members. Today, it is one of the largest churches in Midland.

Downtown

D is for Downtown. Midland's downtown has the tallest building between Fort Worth and El Paso.

Two buildings in downtown Midland are over 20 stories tall: the Bank of America Building and the Wilco Building. At 332 feet tall, the Bank of America building is almost one third the height of the Eiffel Tower in Paris, France.

The Thomas Building is named for its founder, Dr. John Thomas, who used the top floor as the city's first hospital before Midland Memorial Hospital opened in 1950.

The Petroleum Building, originally known as the Hogan Building, is Midland's oldest building. Its unique design makes it the most identifiable building in downtown Midland.

MIDLAND TOWER

Eating

E is for Eating. Midland has a lot of fun restaurants where you can see new things and eat tasty food.

Michael's Charcoal Grill is owned by a former air force pilot. The eatery is filled with pictures and models of many kinds of airplanes.

Basin Burger House is a gourmet restaurant in downtown Midland where they make their own hamburger buns and sauces. It has lots of historic photos of Midland, as well as an old truck out front.

Fountainville

Creamery & Soda Fountain is an ice cream shop in Midland that serves ice cream made from scratch in the store. They create unique ice cream flavors that reflect the culture of West Texas, like Black Gold, Tumbleweed, and Sandstorm.

Football

F is for Football. Football is an important part of West Texas culture.

The story of West Texas' love for high school football was the focus of a book called *Friday Night Lights.* The book is mainly about neighboring Odessa Permian High School, but it also shares stories of that school's rivalry with Midland Lee High School in the 1980s. The book later became the basis for a movie and television series.

FUN FACT
The Midland Lee Rebels set a modern school record in 1998–2000, when they won three Class 5A state football championships in a row.

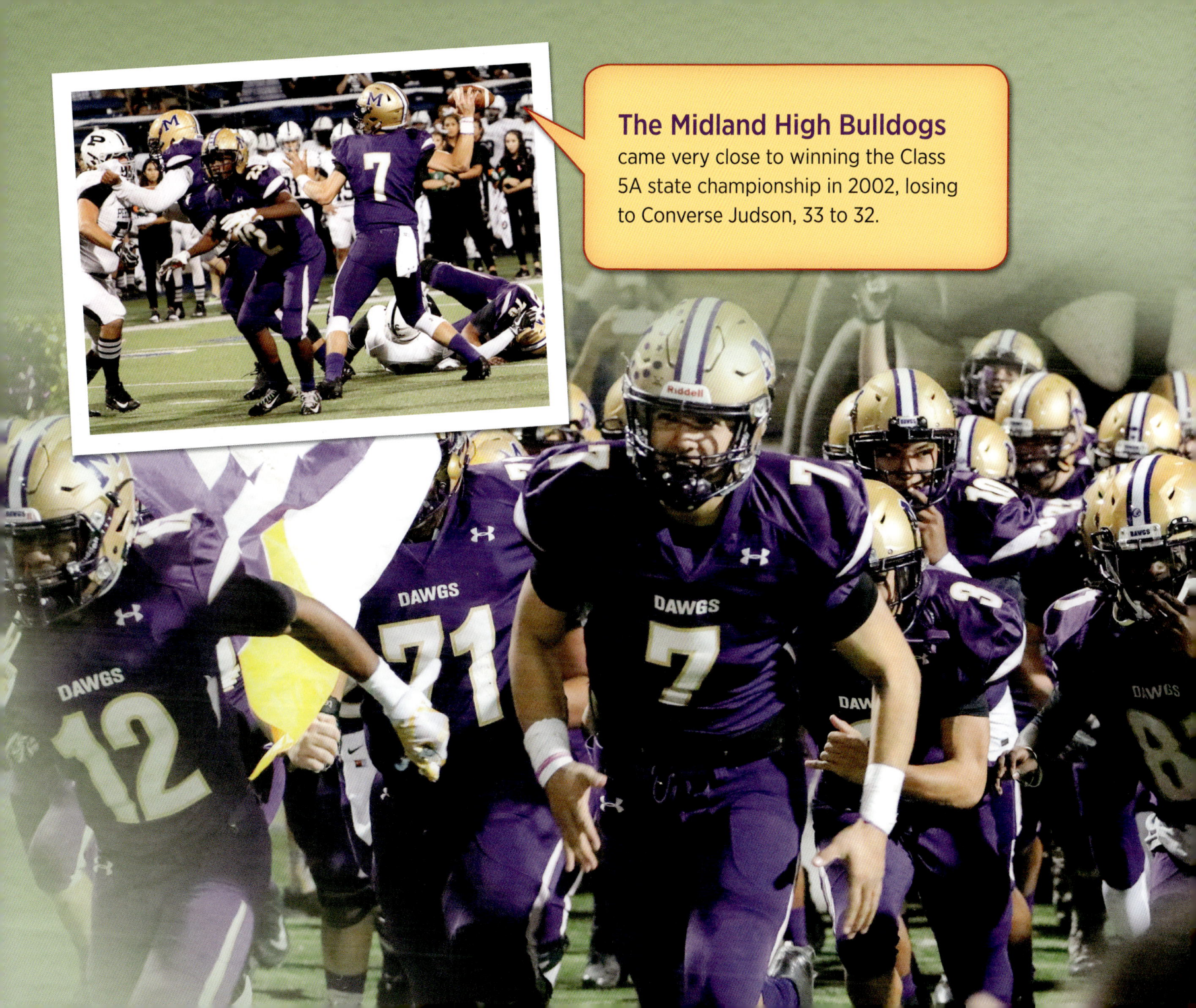

The Midland High Bulldogs came very close to winning the Class 5A state championship in 2002, losing to Converse Judson, 33 to 32.

Garbage

G is for Garbage. In 2016, volunteers with Keep Midland Beautiful picked up 1,500 tons of litter to clean up the city.

The City of Midland Landfill is just five miles southeast of town. Trucks drive in and out of the landfill each weekday to drop off trash that has been collected.

Collection bins all around town encourage Midlanders to recycle. Many everyday items can be recycled, including newspapers, plastic bottles, glass, and cardboard.

Is there a recycling bin at your school or near your neighborhood?

LITTER CONTROL
MIDLAND WALKABOUT VOLKSSPORT CLUB

A PROJECT OF KEEP MIDLAND BEAUTIFUL

Haley Memorial Library

H is for Haley Memorial Library and History Center. The library has books about explorers, trains, farms, and ranches in the Wild West.

The best place to read about early Midland history is the Haley Memorial Library, named after founders J. Evetts and Nita Haley. The library has more than 25,000 books and other writings about western history and exploration, the early railroad, and farming and ranching.

Every year, the library has a cowboy storytelling night.

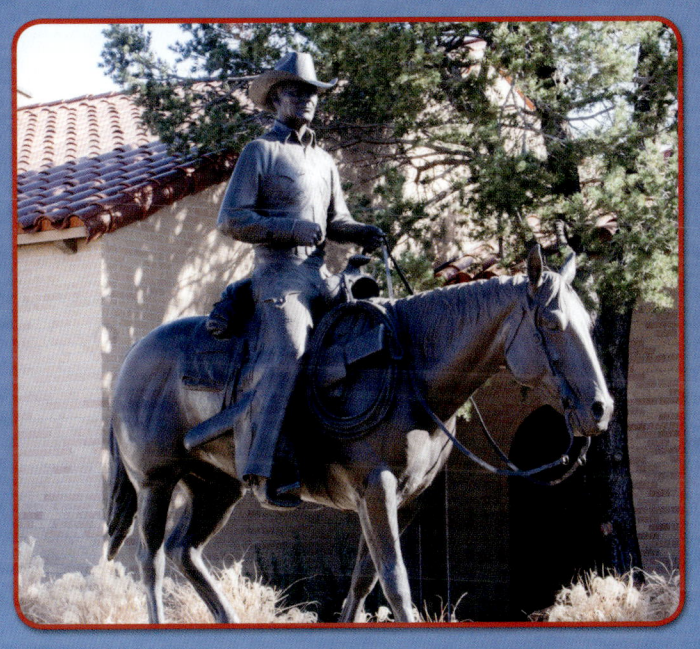

Riding Proudly is the name of the statue in front of the Haley Memorial Library, and it shows what was needed by early twentieth-century cowboys to meet the challenges of cattle ranching.

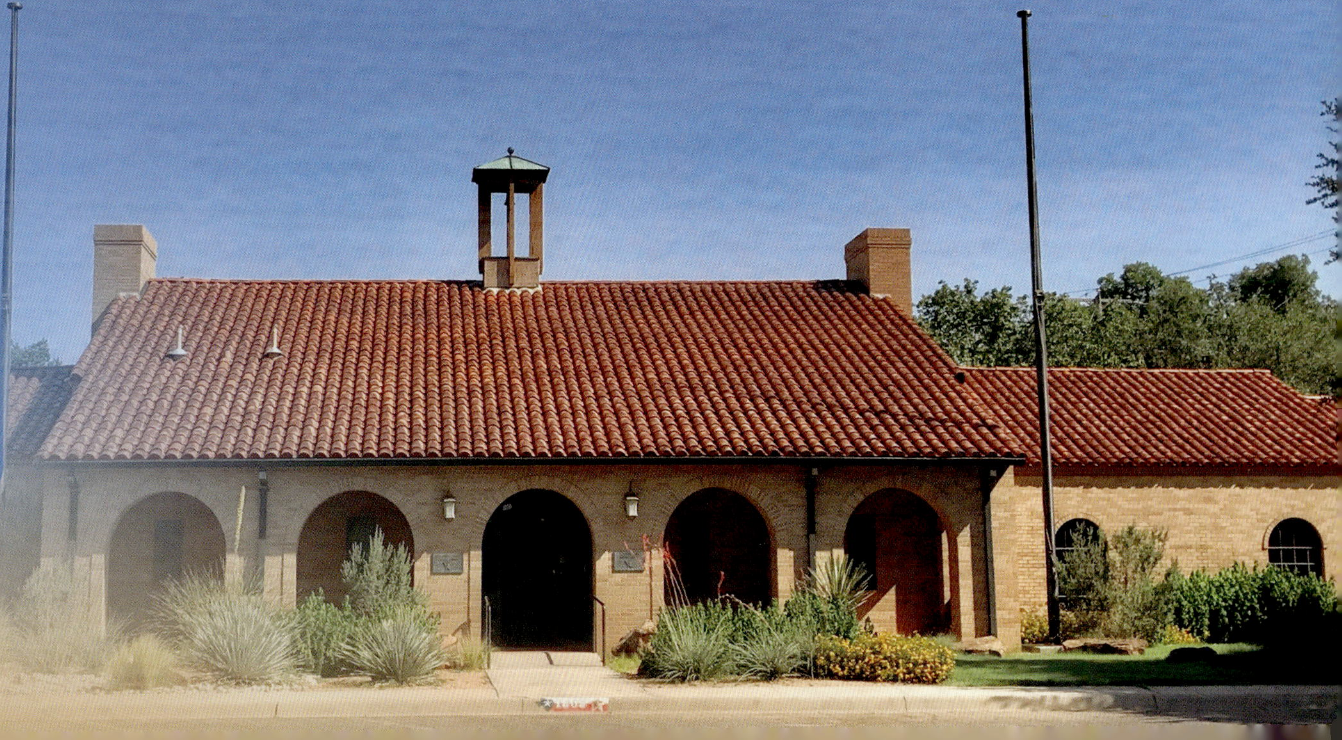

FUN FACT

Movie star John Wayne once said, "If the Southwestern range could speak, it would ask J. Evetts Haley to tell its story."

I-20 Wildlife Preserve

I is for the I-20 Wildlife Preserve. You can see birds, butterflies, turtles, snakes, toads, rabbits, and much more!

Over 400 people visit the I-20 Wildlife Preserve every week. Many walk a trail around the marshy lake, or playa. Volunteers and docents help protect the preserve.

More than 220 species of birds, 43 kinds of butterflies, 26 species of odonates, 29 kinds of plants, 15 different reptiles, 6 species of amphibians, and 2 types of mammals have been seen at the nature preserve.

Volunteers who want to protect nature in Midland have conserved this marshy lake and preserve for more than 30 years. The Nature Study Center is named for Jenna Welch, the mother of former First Lady Laura Bush and a long-time volunteer at the preserve.

Judge John Hyde

J is for Judge John Hyde. Judge Hyde was born in Abilene, Texas, and he worked in Midland as a lawyer and a judge.

Judge Hyde was one of Midland's most beloved citizens. He was so respected that even people he sentenced for crimes showed an admiration for him. Many came and thanked him for his kindness after being released from prison.

Judge Hyde spent most of his career at the Midland County Courthouse. This historic courthouse was demolished in 2015.

"Of all the stories I have either read, heard, or told about Midland, the one common thread that runs through them all is the high quality of character of its people."
—Judge John Hyde

Kentucky Derby

K is for Kentucky Derby. Two horses owned by Midlanders have won the Kentucky Derby.

Four Thoroughbred racehorses owned by Midlanders have run in the Kentucky Derby, horse racing's most popular and historic race. Two of those horses, Tomy Lee (1959) and Alysheba (1987), won the race. One of the other horses, Gallant Man, won the Belmont Stakes (1957) and is thought by many to be one of the best Thoroughbreds of the twentieth century.

In 2016, the Museum of the Southwest opened a permanent exhibit dedicated to the rich horse racing culture of Midland's Scharbauer family.

The exhibit in the museum includes the two Kentucky Derby trophies won by Alysheba and Tomy Lee, and the Preakness trophy, also won by Alysheba.

Libraries

L is for Libraries. Every year, about 350,000 people visit the libraries in Midland.

Midland County Public  Libraries are some of the most awarded midsize libraries in Texas. The Centennial Library is known nationally for its interior library design. This library has shown state, national, and international museum exhibits that many people come to see.

The Centennial Library, the Downtown Library, and the Bookmobile make up the Midland library system.

The Bookmobile is a mobile library. It had its first outing on October 13, 2015, at the Boys and Girls Club. It makes six regular stops around Midland.

Midland County Public Library Bookmobile
Driving Community Connections

Museums

M is for Museums. Midland is home to many museums, featuring art, history, archaeology, astronomy, and more.

The High Sky Wing

Museum at the Air and Space Port has many exhibits of World War II era planes and other artifacts.

The Museum of the Southwest is located in Historic Midland. More than 40,000 works of art and archaeology are located in the Turner Memorial Art Museum, the Durham Children's Museum, the Blakemore Planetarium, and the Sculpture Garden.

The Permian Basin Petroleum Museum tells the story of oil, the important fossil fuel discovered in West Texas in 1923. Visitors can learn about a historic gusher at the Santa Rita No. 2 in Reagan County, and read stories about the 142 members of the Petroleum Hall of Fame.

MILESTONE 1920's

The Marian West and William Blanton Blakemore Planetarium offers star talks and full-dome, high-definition shows that feature a state-of-the-art Digistar 5 planetarium system with 3D capabilities.

News

N is for News. The Midland Reporter-Telegram prints almost 15,000 newspapers every day!

CBS 7 News / KOSA-TV in Odessa has opened a studio in downtown Midland, which is also home to a local news-talk radio station.

With the Internet and social media, people's news-consumption habits have changed, and many people now rely on technology to stay up-to-date on the news.

The Reporter-Telegram

Midland has been represented by a good community newspaper since the town's early years. The *Midland Reporter-Telegram* is a daily newspaper that informs readers of local and national news that affects West Texas.

Oil

O is for Oil. Oil is an important source of energy.

Long ago, the Permian Basin was a sea, and the fossils of the sea animals have become oil. Midland's past, present, and future depend on people who recover oil from under the ground. Midland has long been considered the headquarters of the oil industry in Texas—some would even say America. It is believed that there are 30 billion barrels of oil under Midland and the Permian Basin.

Chevron Energy City in the Permian Basin Petroleum Museum.

Oil is made from petroleum. Petroleum products are in many items we use in our lives, including plastics, basketballs, food preservatives, hand lotions, tires, lipstick, hair dyes, skis, shampoo, CDs, toothbrushes, telephones, cameras, bandages, and many other items.

Petroleum is found in geological formations beneath the earth's surface. Experimentation for retrieving oil with modern hydraulic fracturing, better known as fracking, began in 1947.

Parks

P is for parks. There are 41 city parks in Midland, totaling 1,172 acres devoted to leisure.

Midland has nationally recognized parks and opportunities for everyone, from fishing and dog walking to jogging, sports, and even skateboarding.

One local park is named after Midlander Doug Russell, who was an Olympic champion swimmer and two-time gold medalist in the 1968 games.

What is your favorite thing to do at a park?

Queen City

Q is for Queen City of the Prairie. This was Midland's first nickname.

Settlers named their new town "Midway," but when those same pioneers tried to file it as the official designation, they were told eight towns called Midway already existed in Texas. Town organizers decided to name the town Midland instead.

A West Texas dust storm can blow about 244,000 pounds of dirt through a town in an hour.

Midland
CITY LIMIT
POP. 111,147

Geographically, Midland lies in the Southern Plains of the United States and is located along the edge of the Chihuahuan Desert, the third largest desert in the Western Hemisphere and the second largest in North America.

FUN FACT

Midland has had many nicknames. The first was "Queen City of the Prairie." Pioneers also called it "The Windmill City" for its abundance of windmills in the early twentieth century. And with two buildings more than 20 floors high, it has most recently been called "The Tall City."

RockHounds

R is for RockHounds. Midland's baseball team has two mascots: Rocky the RockHound and Juice the Moose.

The Midland RockHounds are the Class AA baseball affiliate team of the American League Oakland Athletics. The RockHounds became the Athletics' minor league team in 1999. The RockHounds are members of the Texas League and have won four consecutive championships (2014–2017), a modern-day minor league record.

FUN FACT
"RockHounds" is a nickname for geologists.

Randy Velarde, a Midland native and former member of the New York Yankees, played one game with the RockHounds when he was on an injury reassignment during his time with the Oakland Athletics.

Sky

S is for sky. Midland has a beautiful sky.

Midland offers some of the best sunsets in the world. Often, the reason for these vibrant sunsets is the wispy, high clouds that roam above the horizon. The dust and dirt in the air enhance the color of the sun, particularly following a windy day.

Meteorologists say the night skies are more beautiful in Midland because particles in the atmosphere change the direction of light rays, causing them to scatter.

While not noted as being one of the darkest night skies in the United States, the skies in Midland and West Texas are noticeably darker than many areas that suffer from light pollution, allowing even better views of the stars.

Texas Trash

T is for Texas Trash. This is not garbage though—it's actually candy!

Texas Trash is a kind of candy made at Susie's South Forty, a confectionary, or candy factory, in Midland. The creator of Texas Trash is Susie Hitchcock Hall, who owns Susie's South Forty. Susie's sweet creations were enjoyed at the White House during the inauguration of President George W. Bush.

Doesn't this look yummy?

Texas Trash is a blend of cereals and pretzels that are mixed with fancy pecans, drenched in a sweet, creamy vanilla coating, then dusted with powdered sugar. It is delicious!

In 2002, Susie created a treat so big it set a Guinness World Record. Her Texas Pecan Toffee, the most popular candy she makes, weighed 2,940 pounds (with 7,056,000 calories!) and had a retail value of $57,000. After the official ceremony, the toffee was broken into smaller pieces and donated to local organizations.

Unity

U is for Unity. Although they are rivals on the football field, Midland and Odessa celebrate their unity in many ways.

Midland and Odessa have come together many times in their histories to establish programs and construct buildings, including the Center for Energy and Economic Diversification at the University of Texas of the Permian Basin and the Wagner Noel Performing Arts Center, both located between the two cities.

One symbol of unity located along Texas State Highway 191 is a large Christian cross and stone tablet of the Ten Commandments. People regularly visit this cross and the garden area that surrounds it for personal reflection and prayer.

Midland
Odessa

Halfway between Midland and Odessa on Texas Highway 191, the roadway that joins the two cities, is the Friendship Marker. The marker has the word "Friendship" on two sides, and the names of the two cities on the other two sides. It was built in the 1970s.

Veterans

V is for Veterans. A veteran is someone who has served in the military.

At the Midland International Air and Space Port is the Permian Basin Vietnam Veterans Memorial. The memorial features vegetation similar to what grows in Vietnam, a helicopter, and a statue of two soldiers helping a wounded buddy. It was built in memory of all the veterans from the Permian Basin area who lost their lives in Vietnam.

Another tribute to veterans from the Midland area is a memorial along Texas State Highway 191 dedicated to Chris Kyle, a U.S. Navy SEAL veteran who was born in Odessa.

THEY SHALL NOT GROW OLD,
AS WE THAT ARE LEFT GROW
OLD. AGE SHALL NOT WEARY
THEM NOR THE YEARS CONDEMN
THEM. BY THE GOING DOWN OF
THE SUN AND IN THE MORNING,
WE WILL REMEMBER THEM,
LEST WE FORGET.

PERMIAN BASIN
VIETNAM VETERANS
MEMORIAL

Two signs depicting the struggles of the war are found at the memorial. One sign says, "They shall not grow old as we that are left grow old. Age shall not weary them nor the years condemn them. By the going down of the sun and in the morning, we will remember them, lest we forget."

Wind

W is for wind. Sometimes the wind blows through Midland as fast as a hurricane.

Midland may not be called "The Windy City" (Chicago holds that title), but the flat terrain, lack of trees, and shortage of structures make it feel like the wind blows all the time. West Texans often say it's windy here because there's nothing to stop it. So, hold on to your hat!

In the early 1900s, the residents of Midland used windmills to pump their water supply out of wells.

The highest sustained wind speed ever recorded in Midland was 66 mph, observed on June 26, 2007. On the same day, Midland's highest peak wind speed was 93 mph—strong enough to be a category 1 hurricane.

Wind turbines are scattered throughout West Texas. They help capture energy created by the wind.

Xeriscaping

X is for Xeriscaping. Many yards that are xeriscaped have no grass at all.

Midland often receives fewer than 12 inches of rain per year, and its citizens are almost always asked to conserve water. While water is essential to everyday tasks like showering, cooking, and drinking, residents are sometimes prohibited from watering their yards except for certain days of the week. Some homeowners and businesses in Midland prefer a form of landscaping called xeriscaping, which requires very little water, if any.

Xeriscaping saves water, reduces waste and pollution, and is easier to maintain than grass.

Xeriscaping is a type of landscaping that relies on rocks and plants that need almost no water to survive.

Yucca Theatre

Y is for the Yucca Theatre. During Summer Mummers, the audience can buy popcorn and throw it at the actors — a Midland tradition!

The Yucca Theatre is a historical landmark in Midland. Its architecture is still beautiful today, almost 100 years after it first opened in 1929. The Yucca Theatre is part of the historical Hogan Building in downtown Midland and is home to Summer MuMmers, a theater group that performs funny melodramas every year from July to September.

Summer MuMmers celebrates its 70th year in 2018. There are typically 30 performances each summer.

THE YUCCA Theatre was a popular place for traveling vaudeville shows and operas in the 1930s.

The inside of the theater is decorated in an Egyptian style. This was a popular type of design in the 1920s because King Tut's tomb was discovered in 1922.

YUCCA

YUCCA THEATRE

There's something for everyone

THEAT

Maze

Z is for Maze. The corn maze at Fiddlesticks Farms is truly amazing!

Fiddlesticks Farms is a 15-acre cornfield maze. Visitors can wander through the 10-acre pumpkin patch, pet friendly farm animals, and romp through more than 25 attractions that are fun for the whole family. Fiddlesticks Farms also has a learning barn that features cows, calves, goats, sheep, lambs, chickens, pigs, and ducks.

WEST ★ TEXAS

INVESTORS CLUB

Visitors to Fiddlesticks Farms can watch cow milking demonstrations and pig races.

In 2016, Fiddlesticks Farms carved the likenesses of local celebrities from *West Texas Investors Club* into the cornfield to create its maze! *West Texas Investors Club* was an American television series that aired on CNBC.

Midland History Timeline

1881—Texas and Pacific Railway establishes Midway Station between Dallas and El Paso.

1884—"Midway" officially becomes known as Midland.

1912—John Pliska and his assistant, Gray Coggin, complete the Pliska Plane. They build it out of wood, canvas, wire, and tin in John's blacksmith shop.

1923—Fossil fuel is discovered in West Texas.

1929—The Yucca Theatre opens for live performances and movies.

1949—Summer MuMmers begins. It continues to be an annual Midland tradition.

1950—George H. W. and Barbara Bush move to Midland.

1950—Midland Memorial Hospital opens with only 75 beds. Today, the new Dorothy and Clarence Scharbauer Jr. Patient Tower has 474 beds.

1959—Tomy Lee wins the Kentucky Derby. The horses that race in the Kentucky Derby are only three years old.

1965-1966—The Museum of the Southwest opens. Have you been to the museum?

1968—Doug Russell wins two gold medals for swimming in the Olympic Games. He wins both medals by swimming the butterfly stroke.

1975—George W. Bush moves back to Midland.

1975—The Petroleum Museum opens. It showcases the rich history of the oil industry in Midland.

1984—The Centennial Library opens. More than just books, the Centennial Library also offers free audio and video recording opportunities, as well as art classes.

1987—Alysheba wins the Kentucky Derby and the Preakness Stakes. He is inducted into the National Museum of Racing and Hall of Fame in 1993.

1989—George H. W. Bush becomes the 41st president of the United States.

1998-2000—The Midland Lee Rebels set a modern school record by winning three Class 5A state football championships in a row.

2001—George W. Bush becomes the 43rd president of the United States. John Quincy Adams is the only other son of a former president of the United States to also be elected president.

2002—Susie sets a Guinness World Record for her Texas Pecan Toffee weighing 2,940 pounds.

2006—The George W. Bush Childhood Home opens to visitors.

2007—The I-20 Wildlife Preserve opens. Volunteers with the Midland Naturalists, including Jenna Welch, took care of this playa for 20 years before the preserve officially opened.

2015—The Midland County Courthouse is demolished.

2014-2017—The RockHounds win four consecutive championships in the Texas League. Go RockHounds!

2015—The Bookmobile has its first outing. Have you seen the Bookmobile around town?

2016—The Museum of the Southwest opens a permanent exhibit of Midland's Scharbauer family, the owners of Alysheba.

2016—Fiddlesticks Farms carves their cornfield maze into the shape of the local celebrities from *West Texas Investors Club*.

2017—Midland experiences a sustained wind speed of 66 miles per hour, the highest in Midland's recorded history.